Once upon a
time stories
Stage 4

Name

Write the first letter.

Heinemann

Little Rabbit

Skill: Phonological awareness - initial sounds
Instructions: In each box write the first letter (starting sound) of each object.

Join the sentences.

Little Rabbit saw — a big carrot.

'I will eat the carrot,' — she said.

She went home — to find the cat.

Big Goat was — but she could not get in.

Little Rabbit went — in the house.

The cat said, — to find Little Rabbit.

Buzzy Bee went — 'I will not help you.'

'I can get Big Goat out,' — she said.

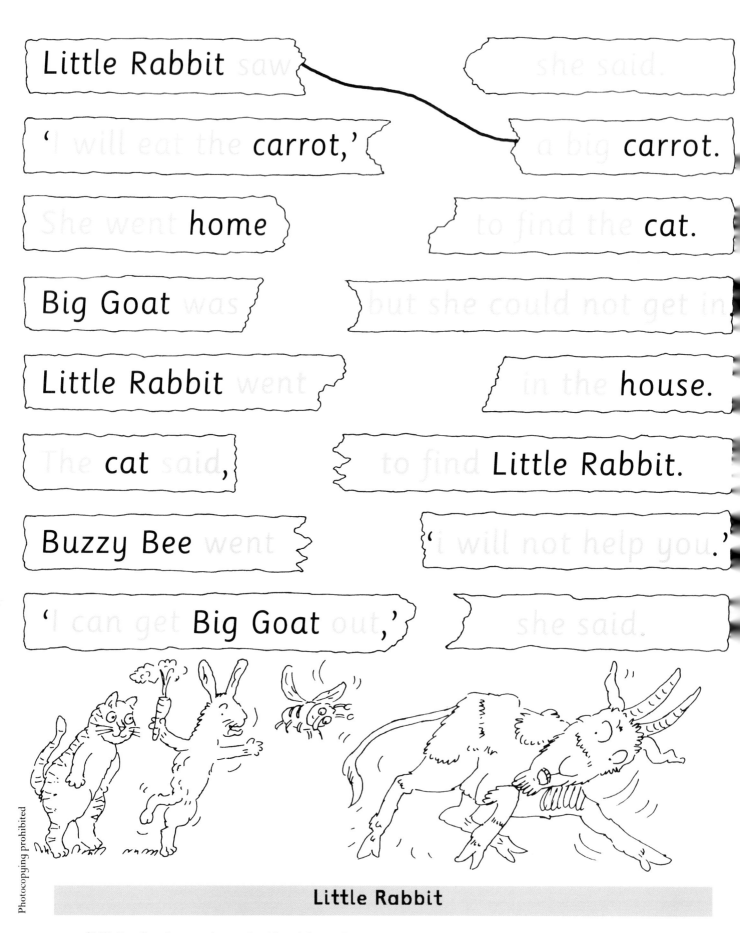

Little Rabbit

2

Skill: Reading for meaning and writing sight words
Instructions: Look back at the story and join the two parts of each sentence. Then write over the tinted words.

Fill in the speech bubbles.

1 The ant said, 'Help! Help! What can I do?'

2 The dove said, 'I will help you.'

3 The man said, 'I will get you.'

4 The ant said, 'I did help you.'

The Ant and the Dove

Skill: Writing sight words
Instructions: Read the sentence under each picture and then write the speech in the speech bubble.

Find the last letter.

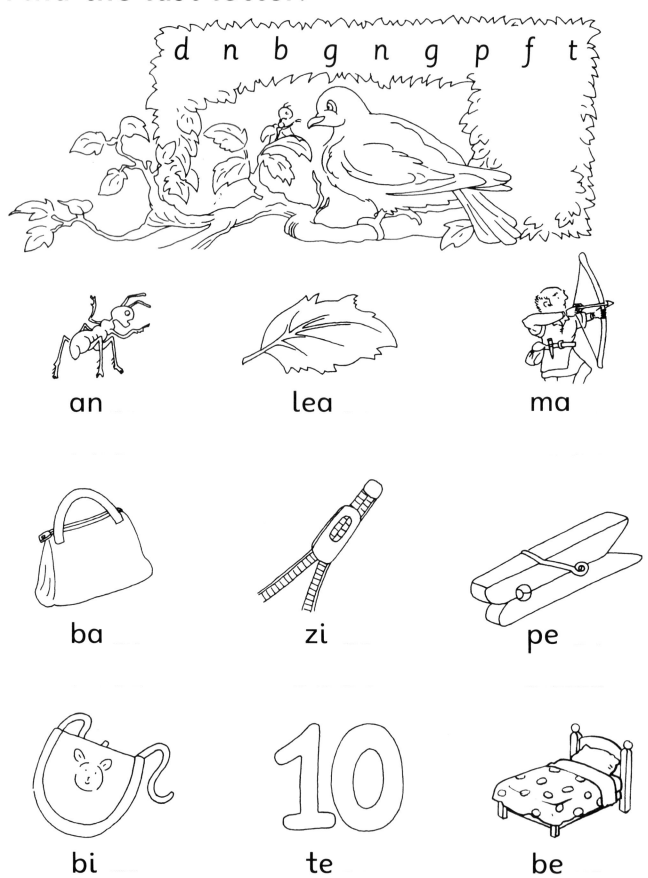

d n b g n g p f t

an

lea

ma

ba

zi

pe

bi

te

be

The Ant and the Dove

Skill: Phonological awareness – final letter sounds
Instructions: Choose a letter from the tree to complete each word. Then write the whole word.

Yes or no?

yes **or** no

Is Country Mouse in a tree?

Is Town Mouse in a house?

Is a jelly on the table?

Is the cheese on the table?

Is the cat on the table?

Can Country Mouse see
the cat?

The Town Mouse and the Country Mouse

Skill: Picture comprehension
Instructions: Look at the picture. Read the questions then answer **yes** or **no**.

Fill in the gaps.

Once upon a time a mouse ____ a little hole in a tree.

In the town a mouse had a ____ hole in a house.

____ day Town Mouse said, 'I will go to ____ Country Mouse.'

'What ____ you eat in the country?' said Town Mouse.

'I eat corn,' ____ Country Mouse.

'But I don't like corn,' said Town Mouse. 'We ____ go to my house.'

Town Mouse and Country Mouse ____ to the town.

The Town Mouse and the Country Mouse

Skill: Reading comprehension – cloze
Instructions: Look back at the story. Then complete the sentences using the words on the cheese.

Add the middle letter.

s _ n

j _ g

w _ nd

p _ t

l _ g

c _ t

z _ p

b _ s

t _ p

b _ b

p _ p

h _ t

The Sun and the Wind

Skill: Phonological awareness – medial vowels
Instructions: Make the letter sound for the vowels in the clouds. Write the missing vowel in each word. Then write the whole word.

7

Match the sentences.

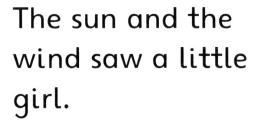

The sun and the wind saw a little girl.

The wind blew and blew.

'Here is the sun,' said the little girl.

'I don't like this wind,' said the little girl.

'I don't want my coat on now,' said the little girl.

5

The Sun and the Wind

Skill: Story sequencing

Instructions: Look at the pictures. Read the sentences. Number the sentences to match the pictures. Then draw a picture to illustrate sentence 5.

8

ISBN 978-0-435091-32-3

Pack ISBN 978 0 435 09131 6

Published by Pearson Education Ltd, Halley Court, Jordan Hill, Oxford OX2 8EJ. Heinemann is a registered trademark of Pearson Education Ltd.